A Pocketful of Rice

Text: Armando Coelho Borges

Photography: Sergio Pagano

Design: Victor Burton

A Pocketful

Luciano Boseggio

# of RiCe

KÖNEMANN

Copyright © 1997 by DBA ® Dóres
Books and Art, Al. Franca, 1185
01422-010 São Paulo SP Brazil

Editor-in-chief
Alexandre Dórea Ribeiro

Editorial Coordination/Recipes
Adriana Amback

Design
Victor Burton

Design assistance
Miriam Lerner

Photography
Sergio Pagano, Flavio Pagano
(for the chapter "Rice and Risottos")

Photography Assistant
Dempsey Gaspar

Graphics
Victor Burton Design Gráfico,

Lithography
Mergulhar Serviços Editorials

Original title: *Il Riso in Tasca. O Livro
de Bolso do Risoto*
© 2000 for the English edition:
Könemann Verlagsgesellschaft mbH
Bonner Str. 126, D-50968 Köln

Translation from Portuguese
Julie Martin in association with
First Edition Translations Ltd,
Cambridge, UK

Editing
Lin Thomas in association with
First Edition Translations Ltd,
Cambridge, UK

Typesetting
The Write Idea in association with
First Edition Translations Ltd,
Cambridge, UK

Project management
Béatrice Hunt for First Edition
Translations Ltd, Cambridge, UK

Project coordination
Nadja Bremse

Production
Ursula Schümer

Printed and bound by
Dürer Nyomda
Printed in Hungary

ISBN 3-8290-4046-6
10 9 8 7 6 5 4 3 2 1
All rights reserved.

Acknowledgements

Alfândega

Leo Shehtman Tecidos

Casa Nobre

Designers

Dino Duarte

Elisa Stecca Design

Emporium

Evolução

Faenza - Arte e decoração

Gea Cerâmica

House Garden

H. Stern Home

Ibiza Materiais e Acabamento

Inter design

Interni - Arquitetura e design

Leila D. Tecidos

Marcia Rolland - Vidros

Maude Monerat

Multihome Presentes

Pão de Açúcar (Al. Gabriel Monteiro da Silva)

Roberto Simões

Suxxar Cook

Via Nuova

William & Gorban

Zona D

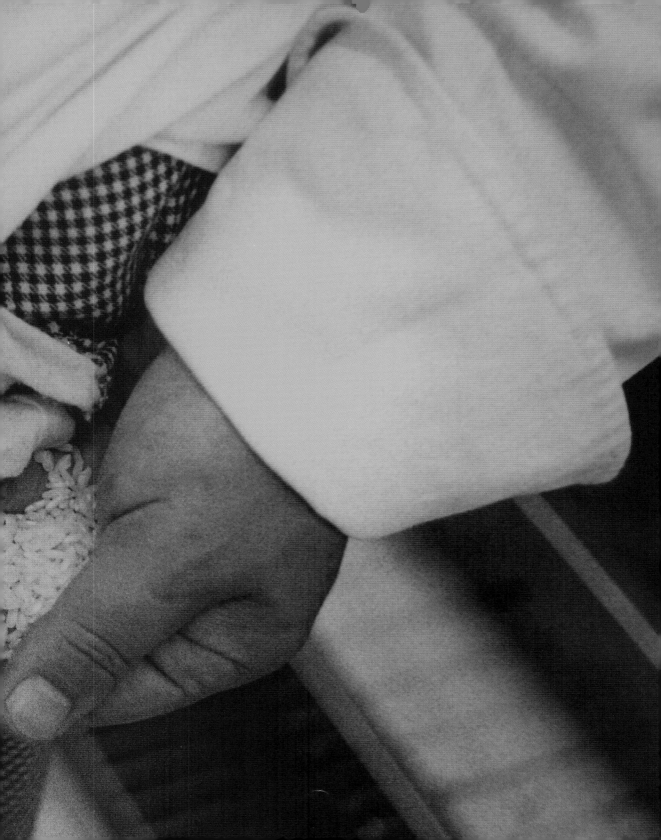

From the sea

From the farm

Stock and sauces

In Europe you hear a lot about Brazil. About the problems, the poverty and the violence, but also the delights, the beautiful beaches, the art of football from the feet of sensational players, the eighth wonder of the world in the form of Carnival, and the indomitable cheerfulness of the Brazilian people.

From my early childhood, I harbored an enormous curiosity about that country which, as seen through the distant eyes of a European, could be summed up in a single adjective — exotic. I promised myself that one day I would have a holiday in Brazil, not knowing that fate had something even better and greater reserved for me: an offer of work from the Fasano family, which I promptly accepted. During the flight to São Paulo I felt both nervous and curious. After all, when it's not that easy just to change your job, what on earth would it be like to change city, country, and continent …

Today, after twelve years in Brazil, the conviction that I made the right choice in leaving my family and friends in Italy, is firmer than ever. As the gastronomic culture of Brazil has grown and become recognized, I have been able to consolidate my work as a chef — demanding and strenuous work, built up day after day, of which the sole recompense is the happy smile of a satisfied customer.

Like other foreign chefs who have come here, I feel that the last ten years have been decisive ones in the development of this art in Brazil, and what was once the dream of a few — like the Fasano family — has now become the reality of many, with the opening up of imports and the growing interest in gastronomy.

I remember that when I started work for the Fasanos it was still impossible to get Italian rice in Brazil, which meant we had to bring it in in small quantities, in the luggage of friends traveling from Italy (hence the title of the book *A Pocketful of Rice*). Nowadays this just sounds funny - such is progress!

But that is how the authentic Italian *risotto* was introduced here, and my greatest delight is in hearing an Italian say that it is the same as he eats in Italy. Risotto is a complete and versatile dish, which may be served equally well on its own, after a salad, or as an accompaniment to meat and fish. Its versatility is also evident from the fact that it is served all the year round, on cold days or hot. And its qualities do not stop there. Anybody can make it — it's easy!

But if preparing it is simple, I can say with nostalgia that nobody makes it as well as my grandmother Emma Magrini, who always made a fuss of me throughout my childhood, and gave me delicious dishes of rice soup and magnificent risottos. I can still remember the flavors and aromas which emanated from the kitchen when this wonderful woman from Veneto was there, warbling a song in the local dialect and stirring with her wooden spoon something which would turn out to be a magical concoction of rice. Today I think she must be in heaven preparing her risottos and soups for all the angels and saints, putting the sin of gluttony to the test …

It is to my grandmother that I especially dedicate this book. Also to my friends and all who enjoy my cooking, I offer this book as a simple present from an ordinary Italian who has learned to love Brazil.

I would like to thank all those who have made it possible for me to realize this dream: Alexandre, Sergio, and all the staff of DBA. But the driving force behind it all is at home, in the person of my wife Fernanda, whose love and dedication have provided the foundation on which I have been able to build my career, and that of my daughter Maria Lidia, who is the sum of all the joys of my existence.

Thank you my love! Thank you Brazil! Buon appetito!

Luciano Boseggia

Armando Coelho Borges

Rice and Risottos

We are familiar with rice but we don't know much about it. It is so ordinary, so commonplace on our tables that it seems a bit far-fetched to be looking for facts and the history of it.

Nevertheless, learning about rice means uncovering a whole saga. It means traveling to the East, coming back to the West, seeing differences which have existed for centuries. Observing man's struggle to feed himself and to survive.

There may be diversions along the way in the quest for rice. And here is the first one: in 1949 a neo-realist Italian film, *Arroz Amargo* ("Bitter Rice") in a plot which is long since forgotten, brought with it a sensual provocation. Generations have been dazzled by Silvana Mangano, the starring actress. curvaceous, 19 years old, shapely legs, emerging like Venus from the waters of the rice fields in the Po Valley. She was the *mondina* or rice weeder (from the Latin *mundare*, to clean), the casual worker wading in the cold water, weeding, and breaking off damaged stems. The memory of the actress's legs in connection with the journey through the history of rice cultivation may be a long shot attributed to the fantasy and enthusiasm of the author. But when one opens up the 790-page tome, *History of Food*, the reader also finds a reference to the film. The author of this *History*, Frenchwoman Maguelene Toussaint-Samat, reminds us in a sober tone that work in the rice fields was never as 'fascinating as the post-war cinema suggested' by sharing 'the superb thighs of Silvana Mangano' (p.156 in the English edition).

As you can see, there is something for everyone. Statistics, history, and sensuality — the quest for rice is a promising one.

Opposite: Silvana Mangano in *Arroz Amargo* (Farabolafoto, Milan)

The world of rice

A tyrannical yet reliable cereal. Not mentioned in the Bible, it reached the West late – in the 15ᵗʰ century. Who are the producers?

Rice was born east of Eden, that is why it does not feature in the Bible. Its beginnings were in India and China, around 3000 B.C., far from the Promised Land flowing with milk and honey.

It dominated the Far East to such an extent that it established a dictatorship, ruling out other foods. It permitted little or no meat and wanted nothing to do with bread, nor milk. Root vegetables were forgotten. Rice feeds and nourishes large Asian populations almost single-handedly, as they never tire of consuming rice in all its forms. Even wine and brandy are made, naturally, from rice.

Fernand Braudel, the great French historian, expounds the virtues of rice in Asia: (1) it needs little space to grow; (2) its productivity is extremely high; (3) it sustains large numbers of people living in densely populated areas. The well-being afforded by the paddy fields may not always have been sustained, considering the poverty and the peasants' revolts, but the rice people have survived it all. If they hadn't, how did they succeed in becoming so numerous?

The East had all of the world's rice for centuries. Its cultivation only spread to the West in the 15th century A.D.

However, even that did not change things. Production in Asia today — the figures are from the Food and Agriculture Organization of the United Nations, 1999 – is still predominant and extremely high. It represents no less than 90% of the world total, that is 533½ million metric tons.

South America holds an honourable but distant second place, with 3.5%. North America and the Caribbean together account for less than 2%. Africa 3%. And Europe, the former Soviet Union and the Indian

Ocean, taken individually, do not even reach 1% of the world total. A few bald figures (in tons): United States 9,603,000; Brazil 11,445,500; Mexico 412,000; Argentina 1,576,000; Uruguay 1,300,000; France 94,000; Spain 810,000; Portugal 155,000; Italy 1,400,000; Egypt 5,900,000; Indonesia 49,500,000; Japan 11,300,000; Thailand 23,000,000; Vietnam 28,116,000; Korea (Republic of) 6,851,000; Korea (Democratic People's Republic) 2,343,000; India 127,600,000; China 200,718,800.

Two or three facts about the paddy fields

A civilization created by rice. An organized and technological society. Time to count calories. Area planted worldwide.

The paddy field began dry and the dry upland rice has remained confined to under-developed areas, although there are still many regions where it is sown.

The irrigated low-lying paddy field is the most important kind. It began around 2000 B.C. With it a whole technology gradually developed. Irrigation and treadle pumps appeared; flood-gates opened and closed; plows were drawn, harnessed to buffaloes. And finally, there is a great concentration of manpower at work. Irrigation systems generate construction work, need watching over and guarantee fair distribution. All of this presupposes an organized society. Where there are rice fields there are people, prosperity, and social cohesion. In a word – civilization.

The paddy-field, according to Braudel, is a factory. Two and a half acres of wheat in France in the time of Lavoisier produced 1,100 pounds of grain on average, while the same acreage of rice could produce 4,600 pounds. The 1,600 calories to each pound of rice amount to the stupendous sum of 7,360,000 calories per 2.5 acres, as opposed to

just 1,500,000 calories per 2.5 acres of wheat. Asia had reason for its choice. The worldwide crop today occupies an area of 361 million acres. That is an area five times greater than the whole territory of Italy.

Food, cookery and gastronomy

A staple food and a culinary one. The role of gastronomy. The cooking of rice in East and West. Main dishes.

How was rice eaten in Asia? Boiled in water, the grains became sticky so that the rice balls were easier to manage – it became a "rice porridge". Rice became the staple food of the East, just like bread in the West. In other words, something which is eaten invariably and daily by the population. This is part of the history of food, or nutrition, but has nothing to do with cookery.

Cookery is, specifically, the art of modifying, of rendering the staple food appetizing. Gastronomy is an extreme form of cookery. With these definitions it is possible to determine where nutrition ends and the recipes which cater to the more refined calls of the palate begin.

In Asia, where rice is the staple, they also developed and expanded cookery of the cereal. To name just a few, but nonetheless relevant, examples: India has *murghi biryani*, rice with chicken, vegetables, yogurt and spices; Indonesia has *lontong*, flavored rice, shaped in banana-leaf cylinders, steamed and cut into firm slices; China heats 'thunder soup' with crusts of deep-fried rice, sizzling on the plate; Japan makes *suki-yaki donburi*, boiled rice placed under portions of vegetables, meats, seasonings, various types of mushroom, tofu, sweetened rice wine and egg yolk.

And in the West?

When rice was introduced, in the 15th century, it was never going to rule the dinner table and become a staple food. Other products had won western preference far earlier.

Even so, rice managed to create a culinary space on our tables. Soya, which arrived far later, has gained enormous economic importance but not achieved gastronomic status in this hemisphere.

In northern Europe the consumption of rice is low and even in the south it is not uniform. France, which is a gastronomic power, has uncharacteristically never created culinary techniques for preparing rice, even though they plant it in the low-lying territory of the Camargue. In Italy, yes, there are rice fields and a cuisine rich in recipes, while in the Iberian peninsula rice has a well-defined place.

Leaving the subject of Italy and Brazil till later, rice in the West has been little involved in main dishes. It is found in combinations and accompaniments. Portugal prepares rice with duck, with squid, with chicken and a further couple of dozen dishes. In Spain recipes for rice are overshadowed by the omnipresent paella. Britain's 19th century involvement in India introduced rice to the more sophisticated diner back home in the form of an accompaniment to curries and as the basis of kedgeree made from smoked fish. In the United States gumbo and jambalaya, Cajun dishes from Louisiana, call for rice and in Cuba "Moors and Christians" is a version of the popular beans and rice.

Types of rice

Differing requirements. Low productivity and quality. Gastronomic arguments which have nothing to do with nutrition. And research?

Rice is highly digestible. It is fully assimilated in 60–100 minutes. Its low sodium content makes it ideal for anyone with high blood pressure.

There are about 8,000 varieties. (And by the way "wild rice" is not rice but an aquatic root). For our purposes, however, the consideration of two major groups will suffice: Japanese rice, with short glutinous grains and Indian rice, with small, medium, and long grains. Medium and short grains tend to become soft and sticky after cooking. Long grains are firmer and separate.

From the point of view of nourishment, productivity and genetic improvement, the **IRRI** (International Rice Research Institute), a center maintained by the United States in Los Baños in the Philippines, is one of the most active bodies in rice research.

From the point of gastronomic quality, the achievements around Vercelli in Italy are more significant. There they have shown that low productivity, far from being a drawback, may be decisive in creating rice of exceptional quality, as is the case with *acquerello*, one of the *carnaroli* varieties, produced by the Rondolino brothers, called "copyright rice" and fought over by the best restaurants in the world. In Brazil, it is to be found on the tables of the Fasano Restaurant in São Paulo and the Francisco Restaurant in Brasilia.

Gastronomy, as distinct from agronomy, recognizes arguments of which pure nutrition is unaware.

Rice in Brazil

Irrigated fields, guaranteed production. The colonel who was king. The Italian who was a good researcher. Cooking Brazilian style.

In the rice fields of Rio Grande do Sul, the curves of the channels made out of sand, the so-called dikes, wind across the landscape, bringing water to the different levels of the plantation.

This layout of the terrain is among the most technical and the most reliable of the layouts of Brazilian rice fields because irrigated rice plantations do not depend on the weather to guarantee production.

Irrigated rice fields in Rio Grande do Sul alone produce 45% of the Brazilian crop. How is this and when did it begin? Although upland rice was planted in centuries past at various points in the country, the permanent irrigated cultivation of rice is a relatively recent phenomenon dating from the dawn of the 20th century.

Frederico Carlos Lang, a manufacturer of soaps and candles, the son of German parents – and coincidentally my maternal grandfather – together with Henrique Moraes, known as "the Sovereign," (an eccentric character who was constantly creating experiments, dreaming of everlasting snow or composing waltzes for the piano) planted the first irrigated paddy-fields recorded in this country, in the municipal district of Pelotas, Rio Grande do Sul, in 1903.

The work of this unlikely pair was unfortunately not very successful. The region of Cachoeira do Sul took over the planting, on more solid foundations, from 1905 onward but the seed was still germinated in Pelotas. Around 1913 the first "Rice Baron" in Brazil appears there, the powerful local political chief, Colonel Pedro Osório.

On the Galatéia Estate, Pedro Osório expanded his rice fields by con-
structing dams, drawing water from the river and the lake. A rural and
urban leader (colonels are not the exclusive property of the northeast),
he was an enlightened entrepreneur. Having learned of the creation in
1908 of the Experimental Rice Growing Station at Vercelli in Piedmont,
Italy, he brought over, at his own expense, an Italian technician to spend
six months studying local plantations, and propose ways of improving the
crop. The solutions put forward by that Italian agronomist remain valid
today, with a few minor modifications.

Brazil is the largest rice producer in the West (and the 6th in the world, with 2.2% of the world total). It is also the biggest consumer of rice in the western hemisphere.

But rice is not the main feature (yet again) on our tables. There is the "Wagoner's Rice" of Rio Grande do Sul, with salt beef, tomatoes, onions, marjoram, parsley and boiled eggs, all finely chopped. And *Arroz de Cuxá* from Maranhão, with sorrel leaves (vinegar plant), grated ginger, onion, crushed garlic, chopped dried shrimp, tomatoes, coriander and cassava flour. And might there be others?

Even so, rice is an extra on our table: as an accompaniment to other dishes or in combinations; in chicken soup, as an ingredient; in *Feijoada* (Brazilian black bean stew) as a side dish.

There are also other forms, cooked Brazilian style and not always original. Rice with shrimp, rice with seafood, rice with chicken and others are being inappropriately called "risotto" in restaurants, as if they were Italian dishes. This confuses the customer and does not promote national Brazilian cuisine.

When preparing rice, it is first washed in cold water and left to drain. Almost everybody does this — apart from the Italians. After boiling, the grains should be soft, but dry and separate. Mushy rice has its aficionados in Brazil but they are in the minority.

What is lacking in Brazilian cuisine? Greater readiness to review and revitalize recipes, and to create new dishes. To hold "gastronomic feasts" based on rice. To write boldly on menus "Rice with chicken liver," "Oven-baked rice" etc., and not to use the word "risotto" wrongly ever again.

The Italian story

Lombardy, Piedmont and others. Risotto is born. Cooking techniques.
Silvana Mangano doesn't live here any more. Conclusion.

With just 0.2% (0.2!) of world production, Italy is very small in quantitative terms, but in culinary terms Italian cooks have raised rice to the highest plain.

There are records in Italy from the 13th century and even earlier, of the presence of rice. But its cultivation only became established from the 15th century onwards. Rice arrived from the south, originating from Africa and the Middle East.

In the north, in Lombardy and Piedmont, the rice fields, being irrigated, thrived. The State wanted to maintain the exclusivity of this high quality production and banned its export. Even Thomas Jefferson, forgetting his position as founding father of a nation, personally smuggled bags of seed to plant in Carolina.

In southern provinces such as Sicily, rice was — and still is — usually prepared in the oven. In northern Italy the cuisine followed a different path from the south. Rice is not put in the oven. It starts off being boiled in stock, and is gradually augmented, becoming thicker — the liquid is absorbed, the rice is more in evidence, it gains in volume and finally takes on a life of its own. *Ecco il risotto!* Behold, risotto!

The word "risotto" derives from the Lombard-Piedmont dialect. It is a creamy "dry soup" in which at a certain point the "wave" is formed which binds the grains together. This occurs because the nature of the rice allows starch to be released, in the boiling, in sufficient quantities to bond the grains together. Stock and sauces are absorbed but the grains do not become soggy. This is the great difference from other forms of rice. This is where the essence of risotto lies. Only the Italians have managed to produce grains which absorb the flavours and bond together in the cooking, without sticking. Other grains, more separate, drier, soggy or sticky – these are not true risottos.

While in the rest of the world boiled rice is usually merely an accompaniment to more important dishes, in Italy it almost always has the status of a first or main course.

At the Experimental Rice-Growing Station in Vercelli, *original*, *padano* and *maratelli* rice are recommended for gratinéed dishes and soups. *Ribe*, which is the authentic rice for pilau and rice salads, can be boiled and stored cold. *Arborio* rice, which of all the Italian rices is the one with the longest grains, is used for all types of risotto and works well

with butter and cheese. *Carnaroli* rice, with its more meaty grains and excellent absorption, is the favorite of many gourmets.

The consumption of rice in Italy is far greater in the north than in the south: 20lb/9kg per capita in Lombardy, 17lb/7.7kg in Veneto, 7lb/3.2kg in Campania and 5lb/2.3kg in Sicily.

One can make as many combinations with rice as cooks can dream up. In Italian recipes the grains are not washed first. Nothing should be allowed to reduce the agglutinative and absorbent capacity of the rice. When the rice is being fried, with onion and butter, it should be stirred continuously, but thereafter, when it is cooking and the stock is added at various times, it should only be stirred occasionally. In the end, the dish will have a creamy consistency but the grains should not break up or split. It should be firm — *al dente*. This is created both by the rice used and the cooking techniques, such as the stirring and the constant additions of stock.

In addition to risotto, there are numerous rice soups in Italian cuisine, chiefly in peasant cookery. There are also a lot of other rice dishes. For example, the delicious rice croquettes (*arancini* in Sicily), unusual rice salads, and the strange Neapolitan *sartu* (rice baked in a mold and stuffed with pieces of veal, poultry liver, peas, and porcini mushrooms, all tossed in butter and cooked with meat stock and Parmesan cheese).

The Italian chef who has settled here with us, Luciano Boseggia, wanted to offer the Brazilians some Italian recipes for rice. The editor Alexandre Dórea had been wanting to do a cookery book dealing only with cereals for ages. They went to Italy, around Vercelli, and from there they brought the right inspiration for this book.

They have been joined by Sergio Pagano, an Italian photographer, invited to photograph the dishes prepared by Luciano, together with his brother Flavio, who took the photographs in Piedmont and Lombardy.

Luciano Boseggia has prepared five soup recipes, six classic risottos, ten vegetable risottos, eleven seafood risottos and ten meat risottos. A total of 42 mouthwatering dishes which both affirm and confirm the vitality of the cuisine of northern Italy and the talent of this chef, its great interpreter among us. The photographs of these dishes and their preparation show the execution of an exemplary culinary art.

There is something missing from the landscape of the Italian plains, where the paddy fields and the rice drills have thrived for centuries. If there are no more *mondini* or rice weeders like Silvana Mangano it is because the seasonal labor has been replaced by machines, as is happening in Brazil. But if she lives on in our memory it is because she is a permanent feature of the history of rice.

A history which records man's faith in the power of the ears and the grains of rice, deemed to bring peace and prosperity, symbols of happiness and fertility.

A history which tells of the efforts and the skill of man in feeding himself but which also describes his inventive imagination in the service of gluttony, ready to trade indulgences for wonderful recipes.

In the kitchen

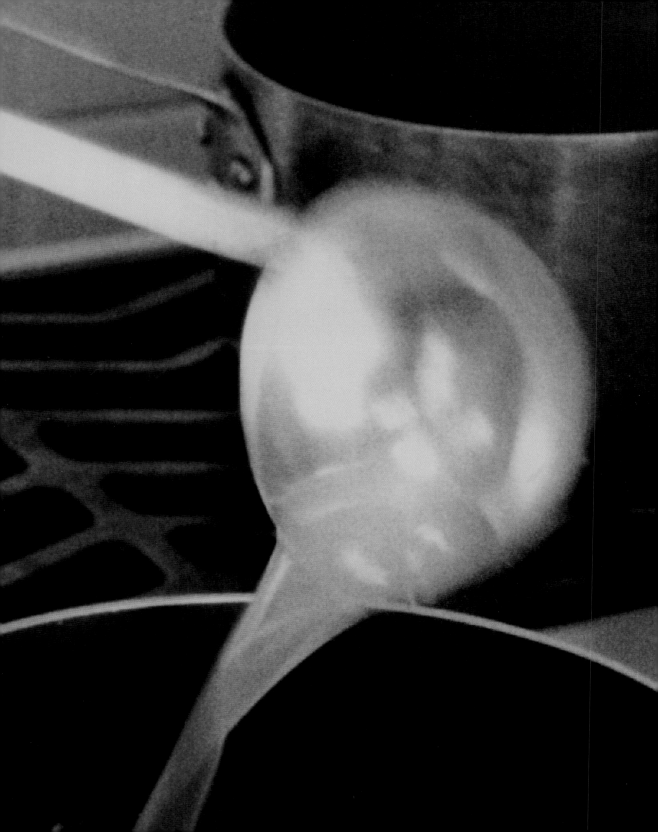

Soup

Rice, barley,

Put the white beans and butter beans in water to soak overnight and the barley for 4 or 5 hours. Sauté the onion and the bacon in the oil for a few minutes. Add the white beans, the butter beans, and the barley. Add the green beans and the vegetable stock. Cook until the beans are soft. Season with salt and pepper. Add the rice and cook for a further 16 or 17 minutes. Serve the soup with a powdering of grated Parmesan. Drizzle with oil.

For 4 to 6 people

½ cup/100 g small, dried, white beans

½ cup/100 g butter beans

½ cup/100 g barley

1 medium-sized onion, chopped

⅓ cup/80 g diced smoked bacon

4 tbsp extra-virgin olive oil

½ cup/100 g green beans

8 cups/2 l vegetable stock (see page 128 for recipe)

Salt and pepper

¾ cup/150 g arborio rice

½ cup/100 g grated Parmesan

and

haricot bean soup

beetroot, and
Swiss chard soup

For 4 to 6 people

½ a chicken in pieces

1 cup/150 g onion, carrot and parsley, chopped

8 cups/2 l water

1 cup/200 g arborio rice

½ cup/100 g cooked beetroot

1 cup/100 g Swiss chard, chopped

Salt and pepper

½ cup 100 g grated Parmesan

Cook the chicken, the onion, the carrot, and the parsley in the water. Strip the chicken from the bones and reserve. Return the stock to the heat. Add the rice and cook for a further 15 minutes. Add the chicken meat, the beetroot cut into strips, and the chard. Season with salt and pepper. Remove from the heat and serve sprinkled with Parmesan.

Rice, potato,

For 4 to 6 people

¾ cup/150 g diced smoked bacon

1 cup/200 g diced potato

¾ cup/150 g sliced leeks (white part only)

½ medium-sized onion, chopped

8 cups/2 l meat stock (see page 128 for recipe)

1 cup/200 g arborio rice

¾ cup/150 g cooked chopped spinach

Salt

½ cup/100 g grated Parmesan

Freshly ground black pepper

leek, and bacon soup

Fry the bacon. Add the potato, leeks, and onion and sauté for a few minutes. Add the stock and the rice and cook for 16 to 18 minutes. When almost cooked add the spinach. Season with salt. Serve sprinkled with grated Parmesan and pepper.

Rice,

langoustine, and asparagus soup

For 4 to 6 people

½ cup/100 g lentils

1 tbsp chopped onion

1 tbsp extra-virgin olive oil

¼ cup white wine

8 cups/2 l fish stock (see page 128 for recipe)

¾ cup/150 g arborio rice

1 cup/200 g asparagus tips in pieces

1 cup/200 g de-veined langoustine (or large shrimp) in pieces

Freshly ground black pepper

Leave the lentils to soak for 4 or 5 hours. Sauté the onion in the oil. Add the lentils, white wine, and fish stock. Lower the heat, cover the pan and cook for 12 to 14 minutes. Add the rice and asparagus and cook for a further 5 minutes. Add the langoustine (or shrimp) and cook for a further 4 minutes. Remove from the heat and season with pepper.

Minestrone

Sauté the onion, bacon, and sage gently in the oil for a few minutes. Add the beans, carrots, zucchini, spinach, celery, and potatoes. Add the water and the tomato sauce. Season with salt and pepper. Lower the heat, cover the pan, and cook for 2½ hours. Take out the potatoes, mash them with a fork, and return them to the soup. Add the peas and the rice and cook for a further 15 to 17 minutes. Add the basil. Remove from the heat. When serving, sprinkle with plenty of grated Parmesan.

alla milanese

For 4 to 6 people

1 medium-sized onion, chopped

½ cup/100 g smoked bacon in strips

4 sage leaves

2 tbsp extra-virgin olive oil

½ cup/100 g green beans

½ cup/100 g carrots, diced

1½ cups/100 g zucchini, diced

⅓ cup/80 g spinach, chopped

½ cup/100 g celery, chopped

1 cup/200 g potatoes

12 cups/3 l water

1 cup/200 g tomato sauce (see page 128 for recipe)

Salt and pepper

½ cup/100 g fresh peas

1 cup/200 g arborio rice

10 basil leaves

1 cup/200 g grated Parmesan

Risotto

Squid-

For 4 people

2 cups/400 g squid or calamares

6 cups/1½ l fish stock (see page 128 for recipe)

1 tbsp finely chopped onion

1 tbsp olive oil

4 tbsp butter

1¾ cups/380 g vialone nano rice

½ cup dry white wine

2 tbsp grated Parmesan

Clean the squid and cut into rings, reserving the ink. Beat the ink in the blender with a little of the fish stock. Reserve. Fry the onion in the oil and half the butter until golden. Add the squid and fry gently for a few minutes. Add the rice and sauté a little longer. Add the white wine and reduce over a high heat. Gradually add the fish stock at almost boiling point. Cook for 16 or 17 minutes, stirring from time to time (as the rice dries, add more stock). Just before it is done, add the squid ink. Remove from the heat. Add the remainder of the butter and the grated Parmesan. Mix well. Serve immediately.

ink risotto

Risotto with

¾ cup/60 g dried porcini mushrooms

1 tbsp finely chopped onion

4 tbsp butter

1¾ cups/380 g vialone nano rice

½ cup dry white wine

6 cups/1½ l meat stock (see page 128 for recipe)

6 tbsp grated Parmesan

dried porcini mush-rooms

Soften the porcini mushrooms in tepid water for 20 minutes. Fry the onion in half the butter until golden. Add the rice and the drained and chopped mushrooms, and sauté for a few minutes. Add the white wine and reduce over a high heat. Gradually add the meat stock at almost boiling point. Cook for 16 or 17 minutes, stirring from time to time (as the rice dries, add more stock). Remove from the heat. Add the remainder of the butter and the grated Parmesan.

Mix well. Serve immediately.

Risotto

For 4 people

½ tbsp finely chopped onion

5 tbsp butter

1¾ cups/380 g carnaroli rice

½ cup dry white wine

6 cups/1½ litres meat stock (see page 128 for recipe)

6 tbsp grated Parmesan

alla parmigiana

Fry the onion in half the butter until golden. Add the rice and sauté for a few minutes. Add the white wine and reduce over a high heat. Gradually add the meat stock at almost boiling point. Cook for 16 or 17 minutes, stirring from time to time (as the rice dries, add more stock). Add the remainder of the butter and the Parmesan. Mix well. Serve immediately.

Risotto

For 4 people

1 tbsp finely chopped onion

4 tbsps butter

1¾ cups/380 g carnaroli rice

½ cup dry white wine

6 cups/1½ l meat stock (see page 128 for recipe)

3 sachets of Italian saffron

4 tbsp of grated parmesan

alla milanese

Fry the onion in half the butter until golden. Add the rice and sauté for a few minutes. Add the white wine and reduce over a high heat. Gradually add the meat stock at almost boiling point, stirring from time to time (as the rice dries, add more stock). After 10 minutes, add the saffron dissolved in a little of the stock. Continue stirring for a further 6 or 7 minutes. Remove from the heat. Add the remainder of the butter and the grated Parmesan. Mix well. Serve immediately.

Risotto

1 cup/200 g vegetables (aspargus, courgette,
spinach, peas, red and yellow peppers)

2 tbsp finely chopped onion

4 tbsp butter

1¾ cups/380 g vialone nano rice

¼ cup dry white wine

6 cups/1½ l vegetable stock
(see page 128 for recipe)

4 tbsp grated Parmesan

primavera

Sauté the vegetables and half the onion in 1 tablespoon
of butter. Reserve. Fry the remainder of the onion in 1½
tablespoons of butter until golden. Add the rice and
sauté for a few minutes. Add the white wine and
reduce over a high heat. Gradually add the
vegetable stock at almost boiling point, stirring
from time to time (as the rice dries, add more
stock). After 10 minutes, add the vegetables
and cook for a further 6 or 7 minutes.
Remove from the heat. Add the remainder
of the butter and the grated Parmesan.
Mix well. Serve immediately.

Sautéed

risotto

For 4 people

1 tbsp butter

1 tbsp extra-virgin olive oil

1¾ cups/380 g risotto alla milanese

(see page 63 for recipe)

mozzarella cheese to taste, grated

2 tomatoes, skinned and chopped

20 basil leaves

In a non-stick pan melt the butter with the oil. When it is really hot add the risotto alla milanese. Spread over the pan to form a cake about ½ inch thick. Brown on both sides, pressing down slightly. Garnish with the mozzarella, the tomato and the basil. Drizzle with extra-virgin olive oil.

Risotto with

For 4 people

1 tbsp finely chopped onion

4 tbsp butter

1¾ cups/380 g carnaroli rice

½ cup dry white wine

6 cups/1½ l vegetable stock (see page 128 for recipe)

½ cup/100 g cooked peas

½ cup/200 g gorgonzola dolcelatte in pieces

2 tbsp grated Parmesan

Fry the onion in half the butter until golden. Add the rice and sauté for a few minutes. Add the white wine and reduce over a high heat. Gradually add the vegetable stock at almost boiling point. Cook for 16 or 17 minutes, stirring from time to time (as the rice dries, add more stock). Remove from the heat. Add the peas and the gorgonzola, the remainder of the butter, and the grated Parmesan. Mix well. Serve immediately.

gorgonzola and peas

Risotto with taleggio

cheese
and celery

For 4 people

100 g celery heart

6 cups/1½ l vegetable stock (see page 128 for recipes)

1 tbsp finely chopped onion

4 tbsp butter

1¾ cups/380 g carnaroli rice

½ cup dry white wine

1 cup/200 g taleggio cheese in pieces

2 tbsp grated Parmesan

Cook the celery in a little vegetable stock until it is soft. Purée in the liquidizer and reserve. Fry the onion in half the butter until golden. Add the rice and sauté for a few minutes. Add the white wine and reduce over a high heat. Gradually add the remainder of the vegetable stock at almost boiling point. Cook for 16 to 17 minutes, stirring from time to time (as the rice dries, add more stock). Remove from the heat. Add the creamed celery, the cheese, the remainder of the butter, and the grated Parmesan. Mix well. Serve immediately.

Risotto with broccoli and goat's cheese

For 4 people

2 tbsp finely chopped onion

4 tbsp butter

1¾ cups/380 g carnaroli rice

½ cup dry white wine

6 cups/1½ l vegetable stock (see page 128 for recipe)

1 cup/200 g cooked broccoli (florets only)

1 cup/200 g diced goat's cheese

2 tbsp grated Parmesan

Fry the onion in half the butter until golden. Add the rice and sauté for a few minutes. Add the wine and reduce over a high heat. Gradually add the vegetable stock at almost boiling point. Cook for 16 or 17 minutes, stirring from time to time (as the rice dries, add more stock). Remove from the heat. Add the broccoli, the goat's cheese, the remainder of the butter, and the grated Parmesan. Mix well. Serve immediately.

Risotto with pumpkin, taro root, and amaretto

For 4 people

¾ cup/150 g diced pumpkin

¾ cup/150 g taro root, in julienne strips

5 tbsp butter

1 tbsp finely chopped onion

⅓ cup/80 g chopped chives

1¾ cups/380 g carnaroli rice

½ cup dry white wine

6 cups/1½ l vegetable stock (see page 128 for recipes)

⅓ cup/80 g crushed amaretto biscuits

4 tbsp grated Parmesan

2 pinches of nutmeg

Sauté the pumpkin and taro in 1 tablespoon of butter until the pumpkin is soft. Reserve. Fry the onion and chives in 2 tablespoons of butter until golden. Add the rice and sauté for a few minutes. Add the wine and reduce over a high heat. Gradually add the vegetable stock at almost boiling point. Cook for 16 or 17 minutes, stirring from time to time (as the rice dries, add more stock). Remove from the heat. Add the pumpkin, the taro, the amaretto biscuits, the remainder of the butter, and the grated Parmesan. Mix well. Serve immediately, sprinkled with nutmeg.

Risotto with basil,

tomatoes,

For 4 people

1 tbsp finely chopped onion

4 tbsp butter

1¾ cups/380 g carnaroli rice

½ cup dry white wine

6 cups/1½ l vegetable stock (see page 128 for recipe)

1 cup/200 g diced mozzarella

1 cup/200 g skinned and de-seeded tomatoes,

chopped

20 basil leaves

2 tbsp grated Parmesan

Fry the onion in half the butter until golden. Add the rice and sauté for a few minutes. Add the white wine and reduce over a high heat. Gradually add the vegetable stock at almost boiling point. Cook for 16 or 17 minutes, stirring from time to time (as the rice dries, add more stock). at almost the end of the cooking time, add the mozzarella and tomatoes.

Remove from the heat. Add the basil, the remainder of the butter, and the grated Parmesan.

Mix well. Serve immediately.

and mozzarella

Risotto with Swiss chard,

Sauté the peppers gently in the oil for a few minutes. Add the chard and the anchovies. Reserve. Fry the onion in half the butter until golden. Add the rice and sauté for a few minutes. Add the dry Martini and reduce over a high heat. Gradually add the vegetable stock at almost boiling point. Cook for 10 minutes, stirring occasionally (as the rice dries, add more stock). Add the peppers, the chard, and the anchovies and cook for a further 6 or 7 minutes. Remove from the heat. Add the remainder of the butter and the grated Parmesan. Mix well. Serve immediately.

peppers, and anchovies

For 4 people

½ cup/100 g skinned red pepper, in strips

½ cup/100 g skinned yellow pepper, in strips

2 tbsp extra-virgin olive oil

⅔ cup/140 g finely chopped Swiss chard

⅓ cup/80 g drained anchovies

1 tbsp finely chopped onion

2 tbsp butter

1¾ cups/380 g carnaroli rice

¼ cup white Martini, dry

6 cups/1½ l vegetable stock (see page 128 for recipe)

4 tbsp grated Parmesan

Cress, ricotta, and

pepper risotto

For 4 people

Fry the onion in half the butter until golden. Add the rice and sauté gently for a few minutes. Add the white wine and reduce over a high heat. Gradually add the vegetable stock at almost boiling point. Cook for 16 or 17 minutes, stirring from time to time (as the rice dries, add more stock). Remove from the heat. Add the watercress and ricotta, the pepper, the remainder of the butter, and the grated Parmesan. Mix well. Serve immediately.

1 tbsp finely chopped onion

2 tbsp butter

1¾ cups/380 g of carnaroli rice

½ cup of dry white wine

6 cups/1½ l of vegetable stock (see page 128 for recipe)

1 cup/260 g chopped watercress

1 cup/200 g of coarsely grated smoked ricotta

½ fresh Italian sweet pepper, sliced in rings

2 tbsp grated Parmesan

Risotto with dried tomatoes

endive, and green pepper

For 4 people

¾ cup/150 g endive cut lengthwise in strips

½ cup/100 g dried tomato in pieces

1 tbsp extra-virgin olive oil

½ cup dry white wine

1 tbsp finely chopped onion

3 tbsp butter

1¾ cups/380 g carnaroli rice

6 cups/1½ l vegetable stock (see page 128 for recipes)

1 cup/150 g grated semi-cured cheese, available in specialist shops

2 tsp green pepper

2 tbsp grated Parmesan

Sauté the endive and tomato in the oil. Add a little white wine, reduce and reserve. Fry the onion in half the butter until golden. Add the rice and sauté for a few minutes. Add the white wine and reduce over a high heat. Gradually add the vegetable stock at almost boiling point. Cook for 16 or 17 minutes, stirring from time to time (as the rice dries, add more stock). Remove from the heat. Add the endive, dried tomato, semi-cured cheese, green pepper, the remainder of the butter, and the grated Parmesan. Mix well. Serve immediately.

Risotto

"fines herbes"

Fry the onion in the oil and half the butter until golden. Add the rice and sauté for a few minutes. Add the white wine and reduce over a high heat. Gradually add the vegetable stock at almost boiling point. Cook for 16 or 17 minutes, stirring from time to time (as the rice dries, add more stock). Remove from the heat. Add the herbs, the remainder of the butter, and the grated Parmesan. Mix well. Serve immediately.

For 4 people

1 tbsp finely chopped onion

2 tbsp extra-virgin olive oil

2 tbsp butter

1¾ cups/380 g carnaroli rice

½ cup dry white wine

6 cups/1½ l vegetable stock

(see page 128 for recipe)

½ cup/100 g herbs (thyme, sage, tarragon, green and purple basil, marjoram, rosemary)

2 tablespoons grated Parmesan

Risotto with artichoke and asparagus

Peel the asparagus (apart from the tips) and remove the hardest part of the stems. Separate the tips and cut the remainder in rings. Fry the onion in the oil and half the butter until golden. Add the asparagus rings and the artichoke and sauté for a few minutes. Add the rice and sauté a little more. Add the white wine and reduce over a high heat. Gradually add the vegetable stock at almost boiling point. Cook for 12 minutes, stirring from time to time (as the rice dries, add more stock). Add the asparagus tips and cook for a further 4 or 5 minutes. Remove from the heat. Add the remainder of the butter and the grated Parmesan. Mix well. Serve immediately.

For 4 people

1 cup/200 g asparagus

1 tbsp finely chopped onion

2 tbsp extra-virgin olive oil

3 tbsp butter

2 artichoke hearts, sliced

1¾ cups/380 g carnaroli rice

½ cup dry white wine

6 cups/1¾ l vegetable stock

(see page 128 for recipe)

4 tbsp grated Parmesan

Risotto with

asparagus and shrimp

Peel the asparagus (apart from the tips) and remove the hardest part of the stems. Cut into rings, reserving the tips. Fry the onion in the oil and half the butter. Add the asparagus rings and fry for a few minutes. Add the rice and sauté a little more. Add the white wine and reduce over a high heat.

Gradually add the fish stock at almost boiling point, stirring from time to time (as the rice dries, add more stock). After 10 minutes add the shrimp and the asparagus tips. Cook for a further 6 or 7 minutes. Remove from the heat. Add the remainder of the butter and the grated Parmesan. Mix well. Serve immediately.

For 4 people

2 cups/400 g fresh asparagus

1 tbsp finely chopped onion

2 tbsp olive oil

3 tbsp butter

1¾ cups/380 g carnaroli rice

½ cup dry white wine

6 cups/1½ l fish stock (see page 128 for recipe)

1½ cups/300g de-veined raw shrimp, in pieces

2 tbsp grated Parmesan

Lettuce and fresh

For 4 people

Head of round lettuce

6 cups/1½ l fish stock (see page 128 for recipe)

1 tbsp finely chopped onion

3 tbsp butter

1¾ cups/380 g carnaroli rice

½ cup dry white wine

1¾ cups/280 g fresh salmon in pieces

2 tbsp grated Parmesan

salmon risotto

Sauté the biggest lettuce leaves with ¼ cup of fish stock. Liquidize to a purée. Reserve the heart of the lettuce and shred. Fry the onion in half the butter until golden. Add the rice and sauté for a few minutes. Add the white wine and reduce over a high heat. Gradually add the fish stock at almost boiling point, stirring from time to time (as the rice dries, add more stock). After 12 minutes, add the salmon and the lettuce purée. Cook for a further 4 or 5 minutes. Remove from the heat. Add the lettuce heart, the remainder of the butter, and the grated Parmesan. Mix well.

Serve immediately.

Risotto with

arugula (rocket) and shrimp

For 4 people

1½ cups/300 g deveined raw shrimp in pieces

3 tbsp butter

2 tbsp olive oil

½ cup dry white wine

1 tbsp finely chopped onion

1¾ cups/380 g carnaroli rice

6 cups/1½ l fish stock (see page 128 for recipe)

2 tbsp arugula (rocket) pesto (see page 128 for recipe)

2 tbsp grated Parmesan

Sauté the shrimp in 1 tablespoon of butter and 1 tablespoon of oil. Add a little wine. Remove from the heat and reserve. Fry the onion in the remainder of the butter and the oil until golden. Add the rice and sauté a little longer. Add the rest of the wine and reduce over a high heat. Gradually add the fish stock at almost boiling point, stirring from time to time (as the rice dries, add more stock). After 14 minutes add the shrimp. Cook for a further 3 or 4 minutes. Remove from the heat. Add the arugula (rocket) pesto and the grated Parmesan. Mix well. Serve immediately.

Risotto with

For 4 people

2 cups/400g scallops

3 tbsp olive oil

3 tbsp butter

A few saffron strands (Spanish)

½ cup dry white wine

1 tbsp finely chopped onion

1¾ cups/380 g carnaroli rice

6 cups/1½ l fish stock (see page 128 for recipe)

2 tbsp grated Parmesan

saffron
and scallops

Sauté the scallops in 2 tablespoons of oil and a little butter for a few minutes. Add the saffron and a small quantity of white wine and sauté for a few more minutes. Remove from the heat and reserve. Fry the onion in half the butter and the remainder of the oil until golden. Add the rice, sautéeing for a few more minutes. Add the remainder of the wine and reduce over a high heat. Gradually add the fish stock at almost boiling point, stirring from time to time (as the rice dries, add more stock). At the end of the cooking time (after 16 to 18 minutes), add the scallops and simmer a little more. Remove from the heat. Add the remainder of the butter and the Parmesan. Mix well. Serve immediately.

Deep

For 4 people

½ cup/100 g squid, chopped

3 tbsp olive oil

1 cup/200 g cleaned raw prawns in pieces

½ cup/100 g crayfish in pieces

½ cup/100 g mantis shrimp in pieces

½ cup/100 g scallops

½ cup dry white wine

2 tbsp tomato sauce (see page 128 for recipe)

1 tbsp finely chopped onion

2 tbsp butter

1¾ cups/380 g carnaroli rice

6 cups/1½ l fish stock (see page 128 for recipe)

1 tbsp chopped parsley

2 tbsp grated Parmesan

sea risotto

Sauté the squid in half the oil for a few minutes. Add the prawns, shrimp, crayfish, and the scallops and sauté a little more. Add half the white wine. Add the tomato sauce, cover and cook for a few minutes. Reserve. Fry the onion in half the butter. Add the rice and sauté for a few minutes. Add the remainder of the wine and reduce over a high heat. Gradually add the fish stock at almost boiling point, stirring from time to time (as the rice dries, add more stock). After 12 minutes add the seafood. Cook for a further 4 or 5 minutes. Remove from the heat. Add the chopped parsley, the remainder of the butter and the oil and the grated Parmesan. Mix well. Serve immediately.

Risotto with lobster

For 4 people

1 tbsp finely chopped onion

2 tbsp extra-virgin olive oil

4 tbsp butter

2 cups/380 g carnaroli rice

½ cup dry white wine

6 cups/1½ l fish stock (see page 128 for recipe)

2 small lobsters, approx. 1¾ lbs each, shelled and chopped

2 heads/200 g endive, chopped

2 tbsp grated Parmesan

and endive

Fry the onion in the oil and half the
butter until golden. Add the rice and
sauté for a few minutes. Add the
white wine and reduce over a high
heat. Gradually add the fish stock at
almost boiling point, stirring from
time to time (as the rice dries, add
more stock). After 10 minutes, add the
lobster and the endive. Cook for a further
6 or 7 minutes. Remove from the heat. Add
the remainder of the butter and the grated
Parmesan. Mix well. Serve immediately.

Risotto

with clams

For 4 people

2 cloves of garlic, crushed

6 tbsp olive oil

2 lbs/1 kg clams, well washed

1 tbsp finely chopped onion

2 tbsp butter

2 cups/380 g carnaroli rice

½ cup dry white wine

5 cups/1¼ l fish stock (see page 128 for recipe)

2 tbsp finely chopped parsley

Fry the garlic in half the oil. Add the clams, reduce the heat, and cover the pan. Wait until the shells open, stirring from time to time. Remove from the heat and take the clams out of their shells. Strain the stock and reserve. Fry the onion in half the butter and a little oil until golden. Add the rice and sauté for a few minutes. Add the white wine and reduce over a high heat. Gradually add the fish stock at almost boiling point, stirring from time to time (as the rice dries, add more stock). After 15 minutes, add the clams and the reserved stock. Cook for a further 2 or 3 minutes. Remove from the heat. Add the parsley and the remainder of the oil. Mix well. Serve immediately.

Risotto with

lobster, ginger, and balsamic vinegar

Sauté the lobster in 1 tablespoon of butter and half the oil. Add the beansprouts, half the white wine, and the ginger. Cover the pan and cook for a few minutes. Reserve. Fry the onion in 1 tablespoon butter and the remainder of the oil. Add the rice and sauté for a few minutes. Add the remainder of the white wine and reduce over a high heat. Gradually add the fish stock at almost boiling point, stirring from time to time (as the rice dries, add more stock). After 12 minutes add the sautéed lobster. Cook for a further 4 or 5 minutes. Remove from the heat. Add the remainder of the butter and the grated Parmesan. Mix well. Serve immediately, sprinkled with balsamic vinegar.

For 4 people

1 cleaned lobster, about 1 lb/500 g, chopped

3 tbsp butter

3 tbsp olive oil

1 cup/100 g beansprouts

½ cup dry white wine

1 tbsp grated fresh ginger

1 tbsp finely chopped onion

2 cups/380 g carnaroli rice

6 cups/1½ l fish stock (see page 128 for recipe)

2 tbsp grated Parmesan

3 tbsp

balsamic

vinegar

Risotto with

For 4 people

¾ lb/300 g haddock

4 cups/1 l water

2 cups/½ l milk

1 cup/100 g zucchini in julienne strips

1 cup/100g summer squash

2½ tbsp butter

2 tbsp olive oil

½ cup dry white wine

1 tbsp finely chopped onion

2 cups/380 g carnaroli rice

6 cups/1½ l fish stock (see page 128 for recipe)

¾ cup fresh cream

2 tbsp grated Parmesan

Cook the haddock in the water and milk for 5 minutes. Drain and flake. Reserve. Sauté the zucchini in ½ tablespoon butter and half the oil. Add a little white wine and reduce. Remove from the heat and reserve. Fry the onion in one tablespoon of butter and the remainder of the oil until golden. Add the rice and sauté for a few minutes. Add the white wine and reduce over a high heat. Gradually add the fish stock at almost boiling point, stirring from time to time (as the rice dries, add more stock). After 13 minutes add the haddock, the zucchini and the cream. Stir for a further 3 or 4 minutes. Remove from the heat. Add the remainder of the butter and the grated Parmesan. Mix well. Serve immediately.

haddock and zucchini

Risotto with

salmon and mascarpone

For 4 people

1 tbsp finely chopped onion

2 tbsp butter

2 tbsp olive oil

½ lb/200 g smoked salmon in strips

¼ cup vodka

2 cups/380 g carnaroli rice

6 cups/1½ l fish stock (see page 128 for recipe)

200 g mascarpone

2 tbsp caviar

1 tbsp chopped chives

Fry ½ tablespoon onion in a little of the butter and half the oil. Add the smoked salmon and flambé with the vodka. Reserve. Fry the remaining onion in half the butter and the remainder of the oil. Add the rice and sauté for a few minutes. Gradually add the stock at almost boiling point. Cook for 17 or 18 minutes, stirring from time to time (as the rice dries, add more stock). Remove from the heat. Add the salmon and the mascarpone. Mix carefully. Serve immediately, sprinkled with the caviar and the chives.

Risotto

with crab
and avocado

For 4 people

1 tbsp finely chopped onion

2 tbsp olive oil

2 tbsp butter

2 cups/380 g carnaroli rice

½ cup Italian champagne (prosecco)

6 cups/1½ l fish stock (see page 128 for recipe)

Pre-cooked and dressed crab, approx. ¾ lb/300 g

1 medium avocado cut into balls

2 tbsp grated Parmesan

Fry the onion in the oil and half the butter. Add the rice and sauté for a few minutes. Add the champagne and reduce over a high heat. Gradually add the stock at almost boiling point. Cook the rice, stirring from time to time (as the rice dries, add more stock). Remove from the heat. Add the remainder of the butter, the crab, the avocado, and the grated Parmesan. Mix very gently. Garnish with a few avocado balls. Serve immediately.

Risotto with
duck ragout and

For 4 people

½ medium duck

1 cup red wine

1 tbsp/50g finely chopped celery

1 tbsp/50g finely chopped onion

1 tbsp/50g finely chopped carrot

2 crisp Granny Smith apples, peeled and finely chopped

1 tbsp mixed herbs

Salt and pepper

6 tbsp butter

1 tbsp finely chopped onion

1 tbsp olive oil

2 cups/380 g carnaroli rice

½ tsp curry powder

6 cups/1½ l meat stock (see page 128 for recipe)

2 tbsp grated Parmesan

curried apples

Remove the bones and skin from the duck. Cut into pieces and allow to marinate in the fridge for 24 hours in the wine, with the celery, onion, carrot, apple, and herbs, adding salt and pepper to taste. The next day, drain the liquid and reserve. Fry the duck in 2 tablespoons of butter. Add the carrot, the celery, the apple, and the onion and sauté for a few minutes. Add the wine stock, cover and cook for 30 minutes. Strain the resultant stock. Reserve. Fry 1 tablespoon onion in the oil and 2 tablespoons of butter. Add the rice and the curry powder, and sauté for a few minutes. Gradually add the stock at almost boiling point, stirring from time to time (as the rice dries, add more stock). After 10 minutes add the duck ragout and the strained stock. Cook, stirring continuously for a further 6 or 7 minutes. Remove from the heat. Add the remainder of the butter and the grated Parmesan. Mix well. Serve immediately. Garnish with slices of green apple.

Farmer's

For 4 people

1 cup/100g fresh beans

1 tbsp finely chopped onion

4 tbsp butter

½ lb/200 g fresh cabano-type sausage, finely chopped

2 cups/380 g vialone nano rice

1 cup red wine

6 cups/1½ l meat stock (see page 128 for recipe)

4 tbsp grated Parmesan

risotto

Cook the beans. Drain and reserve. Fry the onion in half
the butter until golden. Add the sausage and fry a little
longer. Add the rice and sauté for a few minutes. Add the
red wine and reduce over a high heat. Gradually add the
stock at almost boiling point, stirring from time to time
(as the rice dries, add more stock). After 10 minutes,
add the beans. Cook, stirring continuously, for a further
6 or 7 minutes. Remove from the heat. Add the
remainder of the butter and the grated Parmesan.
Mix well. Serve immediately.

Risotto with bresaola

1 tbsp finely chopped onion

2 tbsp extra-virgin olive oil

3 tbsp butter

1 large bulb/250 g fennel, finely sliced

2 cups/380 g vialone nano rice

½ cup dry white wine

6 cups/1½ l meat stock (see page 128 for recipe)

½ lb/200 g bresaola (available in Italian

delicatessens) cut into strips

3 tbsp grated Parmesan

and fennel

Fry the onion in the oil and half the butter. Add
the fennel and sauté for a few minutes. Add the
rice and sauté a little more. Add the wine and
reduce over a high heat. Gradually add the
stock at almost boiling point. Cook for 16 or
17 minutes, stirring from time to time (as
the rice dries, add more stock). Remove
from the heat. Add the bresaola, the
remainder of the butter, and the grated
Parmesan. Mix well. Serve immediately.

Partridge
risotto

For 4 people

1 tbsp finely chopped onion

2 tbsp extra-virgin olive oil

4 tbsp butter

2 partridges, in pieces

2 cups/380 g carnaroli rice

½ cup dry white wine

6 cups/1½ l meat stock (see page 128 for recipe)

2 heads/200 g radiccio, shredded

4 tbsp grated Parmesan

with radiccio

Fry the onion in the oil and half the butter. Add the partridge and sauté for a few minutes. Add the rice and sauté for a few minutes more. Add the wine and reduce over a high heat. Gradually add the stock at almost boiling point. Cook for 17 or 18 minutes, stirring from time to time (as the rice dries, add more stock). Remove from the heat. Add the radiccio, the remainder of the butter and the grated Parmesan. Mix well. Serve immediately.

Lamb risotto with

eggplant

For 4 people

2 cups/300 g eggplant, cubed

1 cup corn oil

1 tbsp finely chopped onion

1 clove of garlic, crushed

2 tbsp extra-virgin olive oil

4 tbsp butter

¾lb/300 g filleted lamb, cubed

2 cups/380 g carnaroli rice

½ cup red wine

6 cups/1½ l meat stock (see page 128 for recipe)

1 tsp chopped rosemary

3 tbsp grated Parmesan

Fry the eggplant in the corn oil. Drain on kitchen paper and reserve. Fry the onion and the garlic in the olive oil and half the butter. Add the lamb and sauté for a few minutes. Add the rice and sauté a little more. Add the red wine and reduce over a high heat. Gradually add the stock at almost boiling point. Cook for 17 or 18 minutes, stirring from time to time (as the rice dries, add more stock). Remove from the heat. Add the eggplant and the rosemary, the remainder of the butter and the grated Parmesan. Mix well. Serve immediately.

Risotto with
veal ragout and

For 4 people

1 cup/200g carrot, onion, and celery,
all finely chopped

2 tbsp extra-virgin olive oil

¾lb/300 g minced veal

1½ cups dry white wine

Salt and pepper

7 cups/1¾ l meat stock (see page
128 for recipe)

2 cups/200 g shiitake mushrooms,
sliced

1 tbsp finely chopped onion

4 tbsp butter

2 cups/380 g carnaroli rice

3 tbsp grated Parmesan

1 tbsp chopped parsley

Fry the carrot, onion and celery in the oil. Add the veal and sauté for a few minutes. Add 1 cup of white wine and reduce by half. Season with salt and pepper to taste. Add 2 cups/½ liter meat stock, cover the pan and cook over a low heat for 20 minutes. Add the mushrooms and cook for a further few minutes uncovered. Reserve. Fry 1 tablespoon of onion in half the butter. Add the rice and sauté for a few minutes. Add the remainder of the white wine and reduce over a high heat. Gradually add the remainder of the stock at almost boiling point. Cook for 10 to 12 minutes, stirring from time to time (as the rice dries, add more stock). Add the veal ragout and cook for a further 4 or 5 minutes. Remove from the heat. Add the remainder of the butter, the grated Parmesan, and the chopped parsley. Mix well. Serve immediately.

shiitake mushrooms

Saffron risotto

with foie gras and mostarda

For 4 people

1 tbsp finely chopped onion

4 tbsp butter

2 cups/380 g carnaroli rice

½ cup dry white wine

6 cups/1½ l meat stock (see page 128 for recipe)

Sachet of saffron strands (Spanish)

⅓ tbsp/100 g Cremona mostarda, available in Italian delicatessen shops

2 tbsp grated Parmesan

1 tbsp chopped parsley

½ lb/200g liver paté (foie gras)

2 tbsp extra-virgin olive oil

1 tbsp balsamic vinegar

Fry the onion in half the butter until golden. Add the rice and sauté for a few minutes. Add the white wine and reduce over a high heat. Gradually add the stock at almost boiling point, stirring from time to time (as the rice dries, add more stock). After 8 minutes add the saffron and cook for a further 9 minutes. Remove from the heat. Add the mostarda, the remainder of the butter, the grated Parmesan, and the chopped parsley. Mix well. Sauté the liver paté quickly in the oil. Serve the risotto on individual plates, placing the liver paté on top, and sprinkle with balsamic vinegar.

Guinea fowl

For 4 people

1 tbsp finely chopped onion

2 tbsp extra-virgin olive oil

3 tbsp butter

½ guinea fowl (breast and thighs), chopped

2 cups/380 g carnaroli rice

½ cup red wine

6 cups/1½ l meat stock (see page 128 for recipe),
preferably made with chicken bones

2 large leeks (white part only), sliced

4 tbsp grated Parmesan

Fry the onion in the oil and half the butter. Add the guinea fowl and sauté for a few minutes. Add the rice and sauté a little more. Add the red wine and reduce over a high heat. Gradually add the stock at almost boiling point, stirring from time to time (as the rice dries, add more stock). After 14 minutes add the leeks and cook for a further 3 or 4 minutes. Remove from the heat. Add the remainder of the butter and the grated Parmesan. Mix well. Serve immediately.

risotto
with leeks

Rabbit
risotto with

¾ cup/150g celery, carrot and onion, all diced

2 tbsp extra-virgin olive oil

4 tbsp butter

½ rabbit (600 g) in pieces

2 cups/380 g carnaroli rice

½ cup dry white wine

6 cups/1½ l meat stock (see page 128 for recipe)

4 tbsp grated Parmesan

2 tbsp roasted pine kernels

pine kernels

Fry the celery, carrot, and onion in the oil and half the butter. Add the rabbit and sauté for a few more minutes. Add the rice and sauté for a few minutes. Add the white wine and reduce over a high heat. Gradually add the stock at almost boiling point. Cook for 17 or 18 minutes, stirring from time to time (as the rice dries, add more stock). Remove from the heat. Add the remainder of the butter and the grated Parmesan. Mix well. Serve the risotto on individual plates and sprinkle with the pine kernels.

Risotto with

For 4 people

1 tbsp finely chopped onion

4 tbsp butter

½ cup/100 g bacon cut into strips

2 cups/380 g carnaroli rice

½ cup dry white wine

6 cups/1½ l meat stock (see page 128 for recipe)

2 cups/200g cooked and chopped spinach

1 cup/100g cooked cassava, diced

4 tbsp grated Parmesan

spinach, bacon, and cassava

Fry the onion in half the butter until golden. Add the bacon and fry for a few minutes. Add the rice and sauté for a few minutes. Add the wine and reduce over a high heat. Gradually add the stock at almost boiling point, stirring from time to time (as the rice dries, add more stock). After 10 minutes add the spinach and the cassava. Cook for a further 6 or 7 minutes. Remove from the heat. Add the remainder of the butter and the grated Parmesan. Mix well. Serve immediately.

Stocks and sauces

Arugula (rocket) pesto

4 cloves of garlic

1 cup extra-virgin olive oil

4 tbsp roasted pine kernels

2 cups/100 g arugula (rocket)

2 tbsp parsley

2 tbsp grated pecorino or
Parmesan cheese

salt and pepper

Beat the garlic and oil in a food processor or liquidizer. Add the pine kernels, the arugula, the parsley, and beat a little more. Add the cheese and mix. Season with salt and pepper.

Meat stock

2½ lbs/1 kg meat (braising steak or chicken)

12 cups/3 l cold water

1 carrot, chopped

1 large stick celery, chopped

Half a small onion, chopped

Salt and pepper

Place all the ingredients in a pan, bring to the boil, reduce the heat, cover and simmer for 1½ hours. Remove from the heat and strain.

Tomato sauce ·

16 ripe tomatoes

3 cloves of garlic

5 tbsp extra-virgin olive oil

Salt and pepper

5 leaves basil

Place the tomatoes in boiling water for a few seconds to remove the skin. Take out the seeds and cores, liquidize in a food processor, and strain. Reserve. Chop up the tomato flesh. Fry the garlic in the oil. Add the strained seeds and cores and sauté for a few minutes. Add the chopped tomato pulp. Season with salt and pepper. Reduce the heat and cook for 10 minutes. Remove from the heat and add the basil leaves.

Vegetable stock

12 cups/3 l cold water

2 small carrots, chopped

3 small sticks celery, chopped

Half an onion, chopped

Small leek, sliced

1 bunch mixed herbs

Salt and pepper

Place all the ingredients in a pan, bring to the boil, reduce the heat, cover, and simmer until the stock is reduced by half. Remove from the heat and strain.

Fish stock

2½ lbs/1 kg fish bones

2 carrots, chopped

2 onions, chopped

2 sticks celery, chopped

1 leek, chopped

3 tbsp extra-virgin olive oil

8 cups/2 l cold water

1 bunch mixed herbs

Salt and pepper

Cut up the fish bones and leave to soak in cold water for 15 minutes. Sauté the carrot, onion, celery, and leek in the oil. Add 8 cups of water, the fish bones, and the herbs. Season with salt and pepper. Boil for 20 minutes. Remove the scum and strain without crushing. Return to the heat for a further 10 minutes.

How to make a good risotto

Use Italian rice for preference.

Never wash Italian rice.

Cook the rice over a high heat.

Add the liquid gradually.

Stir from time to time so that it doesn't stick.

The risotto should be moist and the rice al dente.

Serve hot.